Winooski Motel

Winooski Motel
Black Tiger & Other Poems

By Robert Sieviec

191 Bank Street
Burlington, Vermont 05401

All rights reserved. No part of this publication may be reproduced, distributed, or transmitted in any form or by any means, including photocopying, recording, or other electronic or mechanical methods, without the prior written permission of the publisher, except in the case of brief quotations embodied in critical reviews and certain other noncommercial uses permitted by copyright law.

Onion River Press
191 Bank Street
Burlington, VT 05401

Words and Photographs Copyright © 2018 Robert Sieviec

Photos appearing in "Gulls" from 29th Annual Harvest Moon Ball program, Madison Square Garden, September 17, 1963

Cover design Katherine Sieviec

ISBN: 978-1-949066-08-1

Printed in the United States of America

ROBINS

The robins sing in the trees at dusk and again at four in the morning.
I've listened to them over the years.
While my life was disintegrating I could always count on them to
Announce first and last light, issue territorial claims,
Challenge competitors.

They dart forward in the grass, pause erect, sight prey,
Then pounce!
Older males – dominant for now – chase away younger ones
Awaiting their turn at everything:
Food, mating, little robins.

Robins fear nothing.
Prey is prey and we are all prey for something, whether it be predators
or layoffs.
But if our lives are to be torn apart, we should go down fighting.
If you're willing to accept damage, you can inflict some:
I do not have to win to make you lose, too.

So in the evening I hear the robins sing out the day, another one lived through.
I leave the window open at night so that, at four, four-thirty in the morning,
I can hear them sing in the new one to survive, knowing that –
Whatever time the alarm is set for –
It has begun.

FIFTY-FIVE

I am fifty-five, the same age my father was when he died.

I look in the mirror and see his face and am terrified.

I remember looking at him not long before he died and thinking

How exhausted, how depleted he looked, like a dead battery.

Did he think himself a failure? Am I? How do we know?

Sitting in his favorite rocking chair looking back at me with his thousand-yard stare,

With half an ear listening to his wife go on about something no longer important.

Resting, waiting for his time to come, sensing it near.

I knew then, as now, that it can seem easier to die than to go on living.

Power down, rig for silent running:

Touching bottom, pushing off,

Letting go.

REAL MEN

Real men don't hit women.

Real men don't want to own or rule the world.

Real men fight in defense of those whom

And those things they love.

Real men can cry.

Real men know they will die.

THE MONEY TIDE

I have waited in half-emptied office buildings day and night for
Incoming calls, emails, faxes to execute orders from around the world
Wherever the money tide sloshes up on foreign shores and

Bankers dip their buckets into it, filling corporate coffers,
Planning next moves in the financial endgame where wealth is the prize.
While the money tide runs high, people pursue it around the planet in the hopes

That its waters will protect them, their children, their children's children
Against adversity, world without end, amen.
I live for the execution of the work.

I live knowing that my competence/compliance is needed for salary/survival.
I don't know whether I will be a welcome fit with the resistance
fighters for the planet:
I lack their skills, their fervor, and don't expect to be counted among the saved

When collapse comes.
But hubris may still dictate who matters, who doesn't.
And whoever inherits the fractured future may have to make and live with

Terrible decisions, their consequences and ghosts,
In their not so pure and shining return to the land.
Ask the American Indian what all that entails.

But that time is not yet; the great unraveling has not yet begun.
And who knows but that the planet may put paid to us in one quick extinction,
Killing friend and foe alike and being done with it,

Wiping the slate clean for whoever, whatever comes next.
No-one and nothing lasts forever.
And maybe one day the money tide will slosh up on empty shores

With no-one there to dip their buckets into it,
When the time of Man has passed
And the money tide too has collapsed.

THE NEW CELL

The new cell is sunnier, roomier, has a view.
I drag my belongings along like an anchor gouging grooves
In the pavement, in the floor:
Bible by bedstand, laundry in corner, reading material on shelf,
Bath items 'round the sink.

I sink …
I think about my father –
I remember pulling the outboard motor.
He said, 'Don't drop it!' because, of course, it would be in the drink.
And I said, 'I've got it!' and didn't drop it.

I was afraid of him, afraid to call him 'Dad.'
But I loved him, and failed him and my own family.
Didn't make him or them proud of me –
A poor excuse of a man am I living from cell to cell.
I dream my family together again, things better than then:
Sun shining down on us, smiles all around.
I remember:
Driving the great white whale, the Lincoln Continental, from LAX
To Pasadena via surface streets, visiting my ex-wife's relatives.
I know these roads from years ago –

Always avoid the freeway if you can.
Disneyland, LA Museum of Natural History –
Slides, pictures of us there in '94 before the end,
Before the change that destroyed us, inevitable it seems now.
But was it? I miss my family.

Empty-nested early.

The new cell – sunnier, roomier

Still trying to make amends, lend support,

Sacrifice to help mine.

The Buddha said to me, 'You will never be happy,

Nor will you make anyone else happy,

But I will give you fair weather whenever you travel.'

I'll take that.

GULLS

I

I awoke one morning to the sound of wings flapping.

Looking out my window I saw the shadow of my house falling on my

 neighbor's and the

Shadows of gulls taking off and landing from my silhouetted dormer roof.

They swooped down across the street to tear open garbage bags laid at the curb

For collection for scraps to eat, returning to consume their gleanings.

My depression has overtaken me, run me to ground.

Now when I look 'round all is gray, like a fog that won't lift.

It muffles sound, requires attentive listening to, seeing in.

You can hear truth spoken, see ghosts rising from the sea of light beneath us,

Illuminating past, present, future.

Listen … see….

II

Mother, father, I look at pictures of you, negatives of you in love:
Lake George honeymoon; dad's parents at home; a note by you, mom,
On the back of a photograph of you standing by dad's old car saying
"Jack wants to buy a new one, but no!"

Perhaps thinking about the needs to come of your firstborn on the way.
There's the house you two built we twins grew up in that you, mom, helped build
While pregnant with us; the anniversary cruise.
If I'd known the role I'd play in closing the books on you,
I would never have become a father myself.

Having done my duty I'd have been free to follow the last dispatches into oblivion.
But I hit the brakes too late for generational braking to occur.
There's that stopping distance thing, isn't there?

III

I am eight, mother. I remember you peeling potatoes for dinner,

Good Irish mum that you were.

We were listening to a radio commentator saying how, in time,

People give up waiting for "the right one" to come along and

Marry someone, anyone, so that they won't be alone for the rest of their lives.

Then you began to cry.

Then I knew the choice you had made, terrible as it had become:

To not be alone but to be abused as well.

How the tears fell.

My brother and I are still eight, mum.

The three of us are walking neighborhood streets at 2AM on a wintry

school night

Fleeing dad's rage until it subsides.

We wore winter coats over pajamas, bare feet in boots.

Before you died you said I'd said, 'If you don't do something, I'm going to

run away!'

(Where do eight-year-olds run away to?)

No-one is all bad, or all good: recognize the good, reconcile the bad.

Forgive if you expect to be forgiven.

Father, I forgive you. Please forgive me my failures.

IV

I am older now, past love, past everything, I feel.

I wait for relief that won't come, death that will be late

(Only the good die young, I will be living forever).

The cold winds blow from the north.

There's only duty left: to hold on until relieved and, if not, to hold on anyway:

Holding the line like Rihaku's guardsmen, waiting to be fed to the tigers.

I know what to do.

While unemployed, homeless and job-hunting, I was sleeping in my car at

North Beach campground in Burlington, VT.

One morning, I awoke to see a gull floating down between the trees and

Thought: 'Gulls have been coming up the St. Lawrence Seaway since before

It was called that.'

Pickings must be better now among the campers!

Time has no meaning after all.

V

Memory is a poor thing to glean.

There's what we'd like to see happen and that which does.

Gulls reach inland, sweep over my apartment, following me,

Calling me back.

Maybe someday, somewhere we'll all meet up again where everything

Turned out better, where things come as naturally as breathing,

As gulls foraging inland:

Just living …just being.

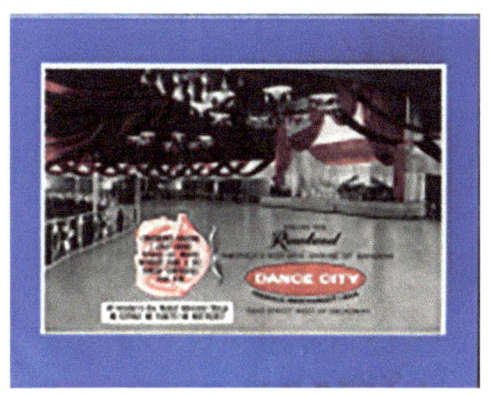

THE BAR ACROSS THE STREET

From me has a green-painted chimney with
Gouges in the brick that resemble cuneiform.
I sometimes wonder if some ancient Ur-person were to contemplate them,
Would he try to make sense of them?

The young woman who lives beneath me held a tag sale today
On the lawn outside her apartment.
She was selling her and her young son's belongings – tricycle, wagon,
Clothes, household items, empty picture frames, the junk of years together

Cut short: her son in state custody now, her leaving having
Lost state help and being evicted.
Her parents stand by helplessly, their love obvious.
Even though I know she made a mess of her life,

I can't help but think she doesn't need her heart crushed any further.
I've heard the boy's father come over, the argument with the mother begin,
The boy begin to cry, a wail winding up, knowing what's coming next.
(Was I like that? I'm sure I was.)

The next day she hides her bruised face while passing me on the way
To throw out the trash.

While the Jews were being gassed at Oswiecim (Auschwitz)
They bit and clawed at each other in order to live a moment longer,
trying futilely
To escape if only at an animal level, for we are part animal aren't we?
Desperate enough to kill one another in order to live a moment longer?

They were dragged out dead from the gas chamber via loops between the wrists of
The trustees and the corpses – a method stumbled upon, perhaps, and perfected
Employed for efficiency's sake.
(How inventive the human mind is, especially in darkness.)
The race is drenched in blood.
It thrills us and sickens us and we do it over and over and over again.

But I am still whole in this interregnum: no bullets, no dogs, no gas;
No killing loved ones to survive a moment longer;
No selling off of pitiful belongings.
I am still lucky.

Are the lifeboats being loaded now even as we speak?
Rome stood for over a thousand years – Western and Eastern
Empires – but fell in the end,
The thousand-year Reich lasted only twelve.

So shall everything we know go, and then us.
Nevertheless life goes on.
(Hecaska wiconi hecena kte lo.)
We are here for those who follow.
(Kici wiconi tuwa icihakataya unk'unpi ena.)

Live with honor or die in shame.
Choose!
(Kici wokinihan ani nains iyo
Wowicasteca t'a. Iglaniga!)

Since death is the most sure thing,
Then, at that time, let us be worthy.
(Kohans wicont'e iyotan wicakala,
Ehan iyowinunkiyapi.)

THE KNOWN DEAD

Like a boat on the ocean
Attached to yours
Whose line has broken;
Like a conversation suspended
In mid-sentence between rooms

That never resumes,
Awaiting a friend's return:
Someone you know dies,
Stopping you in your tracks.
It makes you wonder how

Those who know you will react
To the news of your own death:
Shock, disbelief, at a loss for words?
Someone you once knew is no longer.
Death, once again, is an abstraction no longer.

We move on, our own time
Always nearing,
Especially for those of us older,
Wiser, sadder.
In our hearts we hope

For reunion after death,
But doubt it will be so.
All we knew of those we knew
We knew now.
Our lives crossed here, dear

As we were to each other.
Then – dropping away one by one,
Knowing not where we go –
We leave;
Never to meet again.

BLACK TIGER

(In my dream a black tiger had me treed, its eyes glowing in the moonlight.)

I

Home.
The graveyard was different: an access road had been torn up and new graves
Dug in in its place. I found the headstone I was looking for.
This is what it comes down to in the end: stone for tears; the terrible futility
of life.
Mortality tolls like the church bells in the church in my new home, in whose
Graveyard the Quebecois lie buried.
No Sylvia, there is no great love: only kindness and pity; disappointment and
disillusionment;
Aloneness and loneliness; and in the end resignation and world-weariness
heavier than the stars.
And – awkwardly – hope.

(The black tiger is stalking.)

II

Thursday afternoon; the Mule Bar; it's raining. A UPS semi labors up the
Winooski Roundabout. A group of women are gathered 'round a corner table.
The ubiquitous sports channel is on the TV.
Life has become routinized.
Translucent filaments of her blonde hair float 'round my masked,
be-goggled dental
Hygienist's head as she works on me. (She's so young.)
We discuss snowboarding (on her part); winter bicycling (on mine).
I give her tips on winter gear: merino wool, thermal silk.
(Her hair looks silken.)

(The black tiger is stalking.)

III

Waves of bleakness wash over me, filling me with sorrow so deep
I can only stand in awe of it – like space.
I sink beneath the waves.
I see the sea of light beneath us from which we rose and into which
We will fall back into in the end. Hope is a nuclear trigger floating
in the darkness,
Awaiting detonation.
(You never know where the blade will find a weak spot into the heart,
Slipping in, spilling its contents.)
Sometimes it's better to live without hope than allow it to raise unrealistic
expectations.

(The black tiger is stalking.)

IV

At the end the past returns to take us back to a time and place we belonged to completely.
I am almost done. When I am done, I shall go home.
Now in my heart I want peace.
(Miye olanuns'a yucoya.
Cana miye yucoya, itohewakiyin kte.
Wana mahel mi cante wowahwacin.)
Padding across eternity with the black tiger, moving by instinct:
Waking up, stretching, yawning into the dawn,
Then descending into the misted valley.

(The black tiger is here.)

JOANNA

Joanna came down to visit a glass house and an art exhibit
On a day that was no holiday.
Since she was thirteen she'd been filling the time in
With day-trips near and far.

Remember me, remember me,
Remember me today.
Remember me, remember me,
Remember me always.

(And she said) 'Now's the time if you're going to go,
Before the window closes. Nothing left to hold on for.'
Like mist in the valley the dawn sun sets aglow,
Things evaporate.

Remember me, remember me,
Remember me today.
Remember me, remember me,
Remember me always.

This is the heart of pain:
Loss for which there is no substitute;
Whose replacement pales in comparison,
Even while helping to move on.

Souviens-toi de moi, souviens-toi de moi,
Souviens-toi de moi aujourd'hui.
Souviens-toi de moi, souviens-toi de moi,
Souviens-toi de moi toujours.

Joanna came down to visit a glass house and an art exhibit
On a day that was no holiday.

FLUORESCENT

The ceiling fixture
In the kitchen of my
Distressed garret apartment

Is the same as the two-ringed
Fluorescent GE light that hung
In the kitchen of the house

I grew up in —
Turn it on and I'm
Back there again.

———

Hope is a nuclear trigger
Floating in the darkness,
Awaiting detonation.

———

Kici waslolyapi wocansice,
Kici istamniyanpi inyan.
(With knowledge sorrow,
For tears stone.)

POLAR BEARS

Cry not for polar bears soon to drown:
Before extinction they will fall upon,

Feast upon, the destroyers of their world.
Life clings to life and, in the end,

We will all be looking into the abyss
And have to let go.

RADIOACTIVITY

Life is like radioactive decay:
First the initial burst of energy, then half-life,
Finally transmutation into base elements,
All by ticking atomic clock.

Wisdom and wonder grow,
Along with sorrow, mitigated by love,
In the search for meaning.
Words fail, silence

Being the only response
To digging too deeply.
The universe, better understood daily,
Grows more infinite.

Radio telescopes, listening posts
To the stars, detect its background
Pulse in quasars, black holes,
Dark matter and the chirp of gravity waves.

Emptiness never was. Islands of life
Lie in an ocean of charged particles,
In the gravity wells of their planets,
Orbiting the gravity wells of their suns.

Space within mirrors space without:
Space between the atoms of our molecules
Mingling with those of surfaces
We come in contact with.

We are closer than we think

To the universe: cross-border.

As I decay I hope that

My atoms, in taking on new forms,

Will be reborn in new life

Stretching across time and space,

Listening to stars,

Bathing in radioactivity.

WHILE LOVE'S LOSS LINGERS

Talismans lose their power –
Sometimes the magic works;
Sometimes it doesn't.
Favorite artists fade away, die;
Favorite songs lose their meaning.
All seems as if it had been dreaming.

Basics become their most basic:
Life reduced in its pan to essence –
Survival, emptiness, silence.
Maybe it's best this way.
The emptied life sees deeply, sadly;
Examining, weighing, concluding

That no-one knows what comes next.
We'll find out when we get there,
When we come to rest.
Everything crumbles to dust.
Time slips through our fingers
While love's loss lingers.

SOUNDING

When I retire I shall probably fall into a heap,

Pieces rolling beneath furniture, fridge;

Spinning like coins until ringing flat.

Eyes blinking I'll pull myself onto a chair,

Begin reassembly: reset circadian rhythm,

Equilibrium; change routines; revisit the forest's lap.

Lists: gleanings from the past –

Memories, movies, poems, songs –

What to keep, what not to keep.

Dining alone, seeing movies alone, everything alone;

Filling prescriptions, filling out paperwork;

The mundane providing structure in a crumbling landscape.

Watching Youtube concert videos from years ago

Whose light has just reached me, like distant stars' light

Crossing light years to arrive just now.

Emerging from behind a decades-long persona,

My life is mine again, sense of failure notwithstanding.

Time dilates: I am here, now.

Moving away from ground zero, ashes of the past

Falling all around me; things are falling away from me

Like leaves from a tree, leaving me free.

Pull back from the edge; heal yourself first.

It's hard being alone when you get lonely but,

Once the feeling passes, maybe it's for the best.